Behind the Wall Cloud of Sleep

Poems by Steve Brisendine

Spartan
Press

Spartan Press

Kansas City, Missouri

spartanpresskc.com

Spartan
Press

Copyright © Steve Brisendine, 2024

First Edition: 1 3 5 7 9 10 8 6 4 2

ISBN: 978-1-958182-69-7

LCCN: 2024936818

Cover image: Mark Rothko, *Green on Blue*, 1956. Oil on canvas, 89-3/4"
x 63-1/4". University of Arizona Museum of Art, Tucson. Photo by
Bianca Maggio

Author photo: Alan Hainkel

Acknowledgments

Special thanks go to the editors of the following publications where these poems first appeared:

Synchronized Chaos: "Recurrent I: Walking to New Mexico in My Sleep," "Kansas City Which is Also Overland Park, Kansas: Dream I, "Third Floor of My Office Building Which is Also the Rec Room in My Old House: Dream I," "Motif II: Crash/Landing," "Shawnee, Kansas, Which is Not Really Shawnee, Kansas: Dream II," "Bonner Springs, Kansas, Which is Not Really Bonner Springs, Kansas: Dream II," *Dead Peasant:* "Wamego, Kansas, Which is Not Really Wamego, Kansas: Dream I," *MockingHeart Review:* " Kansas City Which is Not Really Kansas City: Dream IV" *Rushing Thru the Dark* (Choeofpleirn Press, 2022): "Mission, Kansas, Which Also Might Be Liberal, Kansas (and Possibly London)," *Panoply Zine:* "Hutchinson, Kansas, Which is Not Really Hutchinson, Kansas: Dream IV," *Dashboard Horus:* " New York Which is Not Really New York: Dream I," *Windward Review:* "Liberal, Kansas, with Easy Access to Faraway Places: Dream I," "Kansas City Which is Not Really Kansas City: Dream IX," *Ink Babies:* " New York Which is Not Really New York: Dream IV" *Rosette Maleficarium:* " Hydrocodone II: A Suite in the Key of Silence"

Table of Contents

Much dreaming and many words are meaningless.
Therefore fear God.

-Ecclesiastes 5:7 (NIV)

For Daniel, who would have been able
to make sense of all of this

Hydrocodone I: Lord Summerisle and the Phantom Credits

A church basement, I think: the history of this village is
projected in shifting poems on one wall. Brick houses,
all empty now, occupants all dead; Christopher Lee
narrates – now speaking, now singing in a sweeter
tenor than one would expect.

I should be sleeping; pain and duty will not let me.
My part in the village now is to stretch and stitch fabric
for brougham roofs; soft, a sort of jersey, the warm
orange-brown of Hungarian mustard. My lack of skill
and experience will be forgiven, I hope; I am not ready
to join the list of those who were and now are not.

Other poems on another wall; I think I wrote these, or
why else would I cry each time I read the word
                    vow?

I recall books and journals, my name above short stories;
Either I gave them away or never held them in the first
                    place. One journal (the name
                        Honey Mustard
                    comes to drifting mind) called me
                        a sweetheart and frequent contributor.

Another image (mental or wall-projected, I cannot tell)
suggests that I once read my work in the village library,
and this is why I was chosen to remain. It would be nice
to have a home beyond this room, with its pillars and
long tables and black-and-white linoleum.

Morning is here; I still have not slept. I am too tired, my feet too sore to get up for the pancake breakfast downtown. I must look for those books sometime, those journals; if they do not exist, I likely do not either.

Projectors click. Words change. It occurs to me that I cast no shadow. Perhaps I never have.

Recurrent I: Walking to New Mexico
in My Sleep

It takes nearly no time at all, this quick jaunt along
the Oklahoma Panhandle, so long as I don't stop
to admire huge temples of fossil fuels: white miles
of pipes bending upon themselves, bathed in a sort
   of perpetual just-past-dusk not-quite-light,

all clean and humming with no one around (at least,
   their acres of well-lit parking are unoccupied.)

I say
   nearly no time at all,

but it is more true to say
   There is no time to take;

it is always three in the morning, so that I am
   eternally up late but never running behind.

I can never get past Clayton when I go this way,
although I am not sure whether I am supposed to,
   so perhaps it all works out.

The hotel there is far too big for a small town;
I suspect this is by design. Otherwise, how could
   there be these ingeniously (maddeningly)

laid-out hallways, too narrow to turn around in,
purporting to lead to my room but instead spiraling
   ever inward for nonexistent miles and hours?

Someone is waiting for me here. If I can only
remember who, perhaps I will be allowed to arrive.

I would check my watch, but I already know the time.

Wamego, Kansas, Which is Not Really
Wamego, Kansas: Dream I

We have been running all night, west along Interstate 70.
Behind us, mushroom clouds bloom and boil without sound.
       If there is hope for life in the morning, it lies ahead.

Some of us turned north, or it might be that the town moved
south to meet us. Our escape route runs through the high
school –
spacious, salmon-tiled, a temple to optimism in glass and steel.

The music room is littered with small bright paintings, perhaps
nine inches square. Some are on canvas, some on paper; a few
       crack underfoot, like fired clay or thin slate.

Each is the color of those dyed stones, too blue for nature,
sold as turquoise in the tourist traps of northern New Mexico.
This is also the color of the sky just after each explosion.

I met the artist once; she told me her name, then changed it
       and wiped off all her signatures to prove her point.

People keep coming, tripping over me, stepping on paintings.
If I can find the right one, keep it safe, this war (with whom,
no one is sure) will end and our vaporized dead will live again.
       Everyone knows this, but no one will help me look.

Kansas City Which is Not Really Kansas City: Dream IV

So dawn goes down to day
-Robert Frost

South of I-70, east of Downtown – more or less just off
the Brooklyn Avenue exit – the slide rises, seven hundred
          feet of girdered steel and me at the top of it;
this, not engineering, is the miracle of the thing. I shun
          unwalled-in heights, sleeping or waking.
The slide runs away southward: a sharp drop, a brief
leveling at the middle, another drop, a long landing stretch.
The end is miles away, somewhere around 39th Street,
          if my shift-prone inner map can be trusted.
Predawn gray above, concrete gray below: low block
structures to the east, to the horizon, maybe all the way
to the city's end.
These are houses, the houses of the dead.

          All streets are empty; this seems somehow
                    permanent.
          I do not look straight down, nor to the west.
          I am afraid to look behind me.
And now I see myself from the west, from a high
     slideless tower,
               and wonder at our shared bravery.

And now I am on the slide again, sitting, hands clutching
     the sides.
I do not turn to observe my second self, as he watches/
I watch me or perhaps myself. He is/I am to the west, and
          we do not look straight down, nor to the west.

We are afraid to look behind us.
I (by which I mean the aspect of myself on the slide)
have been sitting here for hours, unmoving, waiting for
the sun to
    come up.
It does not always rise; sometimes weeks pass in this
    half-light.
The slide creaks; this and my murmured prayers are the
    only sounds.

This is the only one of me left, the one who sits and waits.
    I know
        this without looking. Now I am sole, alone in
        the city.

The sun rises, gray and desolate. I can see the city's edge
and just beyond it, the shape of the sky over the border
    of the world.
I lean forward, forward, and metal screams in the
    morning wind.
        Below, without sound, the houses begin to
        crumble.

Shawnee, Kansas, Which is Not Really Shawnee, Kansas: Dream II

This is another in a long line
of whole-cloth hotel lobbies
on streets which both exist and do not:

a tile-and-Formica spot
on an off-map stretch of Johnson Drive

(pick dumpy or retro
and either will suit, depending more
          on you than on the place),

and I'm trying to explain to Larry
that I did (eventually) recognize

the young Clint Eastwood *and* the
older one when I ran into both of
them at the coffeehouse in Union Station

sitting at a table with either Anthony Hopkins
or John Wayne – or occasionally but not
always both, though why the Duke should
resurrect for three-dollar drip is beyond me –

and for some other unfathomable reason
James Urbaniak, thin and vaguely dangerous,
who smirked at all of us and left halfway
          through the conversation.

Larry all the while fiddles with his phone,
poking it with a little screwdriver,
only making appropriate noises so as
             to seem engaged,

so I walk out into a half-dawn of
backlit plastic, oddly angled streets
             and lumen-polluted overcast.

I suppose I might eventually find my way
             back to the map and home –

that, or just go upstairs and fall into dream
within dream, still in my clothes on
forty dollars' worth of rented sheets.

Don't press me for a clear answer; I am and
will be asleep the whole sometime.

Belle, Missouri, Which is Not Really
Belle, Missouri: Dream I

(on the eve of John Dorsey's cancer surgery)

John cries out in his sleep, and we who keep watch
over him pace the cold plank floor and redouble
our vigilance against intrusions, cold bureaucrats,
            dutiful angels on grim missions.

The moon wobbles in its course, blinks and sputters;
Baldinger ascends to the heavens in the bed of a
blue dump truck, screws it back into the firmament,
slides down, scatters the rest of us into a 7-10 split.

Dawn now, all cool pink and gray with fog soothing
the hills; John joins us on the front porch, holding
silent court from a metal folding chair, and God's eye
            flashes from every drop of dew.

Mission, Kansas, Which Also Might Be Liberal, Kansas (and Possibly London): Dream I

A predawn Sunday walk to retrieve my son
from a friend's house, but a high school acting
troupe (possibly his, though just as likely young
strangers) bar my way, bidding me play a part:

a suspect – suspected of what, no one will say –
held at close-range gunpoint, one barrel behind
the right ear and the other between the eyes, each
muzzle a cough or twitch away from denting skin.

Ten seconds in silence, twenty, and the scene
grows tiresome, in need of a shakeup. On a whim,
I snatch and grab the eye-level revolver, mime
taking out both captors; they giggle and concede.

Having earned both release and (it seems) respect,
I hit the street again. One block of it seems to run
near a softball field named for a hometown oil
millionaire, but the structure itself is blurred,

a landmark in witness protection; then all shifts,
and I see the suburban split-level where I hope
to find my son. I have forgotten the address, as
well as the last name of the friend hosting him.

I find him taking out the trash in gray almost-
morning light; he seems annoyed at my presence,
tells me to go on to church without him; a time
for his return home is waved away, undefined.

My father, returned to life after more than two
decades, waits for me at what seems to be a
long concourse at Heathrow; services take place
in glassed-off booths, where two or more gather

to contemplate departures from the Way and pray
for smooth flight to the World to Come. Our stall
is shared by an artist, a woman whose name also
eludes me, though I resent her presence for no

reason I am able to identify. Rather than stay to
meditate on this bit of uncharity, I wander to a
supply closet, taking out another prop pistol and
a handful of small beads in brown, orange and tan.

These should serve as the makings of something
profound, or might were I not suddenly distracted
by the television in the contemplation booth; my
son is on the news, looking younger by a dozen

years or more. His host (or perhaps new) family
laud basketball prowess, which I have not seen
before: he dunks on their son with raw grace. He
looks happy; I must live with the pain of his grin.

Mission, Kansas, Suddenly Taken Out of a Slain World: Dream I

In the southwestern sky, orange light – a second setting
   sun –
descends at a shallow angle; there is no sound of
   impact, only
a ball of doom-colored light, shot through with seven
   thunders,
expanding, fading. All falls into calm, lying gray twilight
   and
          there is silence in earth and Heaven for half a
   breath.

From high ground (or perhaps it is that all toward the
   landfall
has been pushed into the abyss) I watch blocks and
   subdivisions
blaze up methodically; flames consume Lenexa, the
   ever-clogged
          69 Highway interchange, Antioch Park, my
   office building.

All shifts to deep pine forest at near-dawn, and I am
   hunted; men in
dark clothing, spotlights and voices tearing through
   trees, through
          fog, through my hopes of escape into this
   new wherever.

Now a street unconnected to any other, one house on
    each side;
I take refuge with seminarians, their missionary plans
    wrecked
        as whatever lies out there beyond the enveloping
    mist.

From the other house, an ultimatum: I am to surrender
    myself
by one in the afternoon, or I will not be the only one
    annihilated.
My sanctuary sprouts new rooms behind every door,
    though none
        offers a guaranteed place of hiding; I must make
    my peace.

Standing on the front porch, I see the sun break through;
    it is a
small comfort, a sign that life of some sort can go on,
    even if
confined to this microcosmic remnant. I chant a prayer
    in the
tongue of angels and answer myself from the top window
    of
        the other house; we have been resentenced to live.

Motif II: Crash/Landing
(A Semi-Tragedy in Two Acts)

I. On the south side of Liberal, Kansas

For some reason, we all know to gather along the old
highway just north of where it meets the bypass; between
them, a wedge

       of dry prairie grass anticipates dawn and
something else.

The plane comes in from the south: long, thin, white,
    unliveried.
(Picture the offspring of a Concorde and a 707, its father's
    nose

       and its mother's wings, and you have it close
enough.)

Gear still retracted, it slides in and turns top, three perfect
spins down the field without bending so much as one thin
dun blade;

       there is no sound but breaths all drawn in at once.

No flame, no laceration of aluminum skin, not so much
as a cloud of honest Kansas dust; nose pointed back
where it came from,

       the plane rests unperturbed, maiden-flight pristine.

From somewhere in the crowd, a Panhandle-tinged twang:
       Well, that ol' boy done 'er again, didn't he? Might
       as well go see what all he brung us this time.

II. Manhattan, Kansas, on the street where Jim Roper lived

Stuffed with burgers (eaten, as ever, standing in the
kitchen), we walk north toward the football stadium,
discussing the quarterback situation and whether
threatened rain will hold off.

Someone – probably Gary – brings up a years-ago summer
solstice party, the honey-haired girl nobody knew who
showed up in a toga and antler-danced with Jim in the
living room.

This is routine, ritual, sacrament, not to be disturbed by
anything like that belly-flopping 747 two blocks ahead,
plunging into low brick blocks where married students live.

Impact now, an infrabass thump and rumble. A fireball races
to consume families, tricycles, maples, all of us. It is red
and orange and beautiful; I breathe in and am not afraid.

Hutchinson, Kansas, Which is Not Really
Hutchinson, Kansas: Dream IV

We have come to get out of the city,
visit old friends and our former church,
only to find the town shadowed by this
simulated mushroom cloud and heavy
equipment – bulldozers, backhoes, an
occasional dump truck – rattle-rolling
through the streets outside this hotel
coffee shop as we linger over breakfast.

It is a war exercise, we are told, one
known to the locals; perhaps all this
plays out across the country today,
unannounced and ominous. We sit
three blocks from Ground Zero, or
where a computer says it would be.

> *Ten thousand, one hundred*
> *and eighty-two dead, they say,*
> *but I guess that's all pretend,*

our waitress informs us and tops off
my coffee as another dozer rolls by.

I wonder if we are among them;
surely someone would have told us
before we ordered, as no one would
want even faux casualties eating up
the food. Ham and eggs aren't cheap.

Outside, the cloud holds its shape,
no mean feat in the Kansas wind.

> *Some poor sucker had to*
> *put that up, and another*
> *one's gonna have to take*
> *it down when this is over,*

the waitress muses to no one but
the front window.

> *Not sure who's paying for*
> *all this, but it's probably me.*

Bonner Springs, Kansas, Which is Not Really
Bonner Springs, Kansas: Dream II

The stakeout is just beginning. I have time to go for
    coffee.
The town's heart is only a few blocks south; its buildings
are taller than I remember, but this bodes well; somewhere
in this tangle of five-story limestone, there must be a
    place.

The sidewalk spans a ravine, brush-lined, hundreds of
    feet
deep. There is no handrail, and the walkway is less than
a yard wide. I take no shame in dropping to my knees
to cross, but a man on the other side rolls his eyes and
tosses a few
        dead dogwood branches to impede my way.

No need; I am being called back. We have been made.
    Our
        target has seen telltale peanuts floating in his
    gutter.

(He looks like a television character actor of some minor
note, one who always seems to play a well-meaning but
largely incompetent foil to the protagonist. I will
    remember
his name someday, likely on my deathbed, and my loved
    ones
        will always wonder why those were my last
words.)

We will have to take another tack, so we roll back into the city along Kaw Drive. I see a coffeehouse, set back among trees on the north side of the road. We do not stop.

Shawnee, Kansas After Yet Another
Apocalypse: Dream I

Yesterday, a lost nuclear exchange (with
New Zealand, of all people, and no one
                is sure just what set it all off);

we have fled home safely from the Tetons,
all roads undulating over new hills along
the way. Somewhere in the Nebraska
Panhandle, I fell into a dream of all my
other lives and their wrenching ends.

Today, I need only say my name, and all
disparagements of God's Anointed Leader
(no matter how privately muttered) appear
on video screens around the ashed city.

I suppose I should be glad for the sudden
depopulation; fewer eyes on my asides
and wisecracks, though shame seems to
                be the only punishment applied.

Perhaps church will offer solace (even
sanctuary within the sanctuary, if things
should come to the usual All That); at
the very least, the service should give,
if not peace, then at least some passing
understanding of the narrow way forward.

I have forgotten the words to my solo,
or that I was supposed to sing one in
the first place; blame it on the war, but
I still must sing my piece or cry trying.

Third Floor of My Office Building Which is
Also the Rec Room in My Old House:
Dream I

It all started downstairs, an offhand Nerf ball dunk
on an eight-foot plastic rim; I hung in the air just
long enough to estimate the gap from soles to floor.

Now, with an audience and a high ceiling, I have
decided to give this new ability a full workout.

First rising to tiptoe, as men in my family always
do in times of urgency or strong emotion, I bounce
twice on the balls of my feet, then swing arms back
forward up and rise – less a true leap than pushing
off from the bottom of a pool, letting buoyancy
do the work. I latch on to a rafter by my fingertips,
swaying in the faint breeze of fans electric and human.

A high-pitched sound in my ear; somehow I know –
an instinct born in my late middle age – that this is
not the ringing born of jamming my head into my
favorite bar band's speakers back when that sort of
thing made Coors-Light-and-idiocy-fueled sense.

This is the song of air in my lungs, air lighter than
itself, and when I release it all and take in new breath,
I will be floorbound again, and old, and ordinary.

My landing is slow, soft; I inhale deeply, prepare for
        another takeoff, but all novelty has worn off.

My colleagues disperse, reoccupied by meetings
and deadlines. I should go to lunch soon, I suppose –
but first, let me rise one last time, be more than
what reality allows. (Just one more last time.)

Perhaps I can master a sort of hovering swim, shoot
a game of eight-ball against myself without ever
touching the floor. Slop counts, or at least until I
get the hang of hanging at the proper height.

What else is one to do on a Friday, the codes of
          dress and gravity both suspended with pay?

New York Which is Not Really New York: Dream I

North of Central Park, the city slopes upward
toward Harlem; its streets and sidewalks are
empty, and someone has taken down all signs.

I wait for someone, knowing and not knowing
whom, in the only place which is not closed:
a tiled, high-ceilinged lunch counter, where the
uniformed counterman silently takes my order.

The hamburger is better than passable, though
when I look away it heals itself of each bite: I
must not let myself get distracted, or I will be
here all afternoon and eat myself into nausea.

When I finish, even the counterman is gone.
A walk around the block to get my bearings
does no good; when I return even the lunch
counter has vanished. Perhaps it was never
there in the first place; these things happen.

There are sounds of excitement toward the
south and east, the first human noises of the
day. They grow louder east of the park, and
afternoon rolls back to bright midmorning.

I join a crowd moving farther south and east;
some chatter in anticipation, while others
begin to cry as we enter an open space.

This is what awaits those of us who have
not turned back in fear or fatigue: a flood
wall, high as a football field is long, covered
in bright green grass. Below, a gray X of
concrete divides a wide flat treeless lawn.

We have brought folding chairs; we set them
up facing east, sit with faces toward the wall.
It is a pleasant nondescript day to die, though
no one speaks of that or anything else.

We all wear brightly colored hats: I cannot see mine,
because it will not come off. I think it is red,
a pillbox my mother left in this or that closet
                when we moved to the country.

The first wave strikes, flings spray a mile in the air.
                The second begins to overtop the wall.

The water is black; things with teeth move in it.
                I wish I had brought a book.

Lee's Summit, Missouri, Which is Not Really Lee's Summit, Missouri: Dream I

I saw two police cars earlier, pulling off the interstate;
        I cannot linger. The rules are simple:

> *Enter only the back yards with fish ponds. Do not look
> at the fish. If birds or squirrels attempt to speak to you,
> listen but do not respond. Carry cardboard at all times,
> a flattened box that might once have held a microwave
> oven or a weighted blanket.*

One time around each pond usually suffices to tell me
what I need to know, even if I have no idea what that
might be. If anyone asks, though no one ever has, I am
doing a security check for the homeowners' association.

If it begins to rain, I will be allowed to go home. If I am
arrested, or about to be, I will be allowed to wake up.

Motif I: The Odd of Mall Things

I. Perth, Western Australia to Kansas City

The boardwalk meanders away, west-northwest;
given a day, one might walk around the continent –
but only in that direction, and only if one avoids
detours. Turning right at Darwin, trying to dodge a
crocodile, I find myself two seasons and as many
hemispheres away, stuck in the parking lot of a
   Honda dealership somewhere in Northtown.

Might as well cross the street, if I can find an exit,
and see what's in the cutout bin at the record store.
No point in trying to retrace my steps; the path back
is nowhere to be found now, and Australia will be
   closed at this hour anyway.

II. Either Shawnee or Overland Park, Kansas

No coffee to be had, apparently, because the safe
in the place next to the bookstore is locked until
Monday; we find ourselves wandering in the lower
level, where the path slopes downward past busy
   clothing stores in which nothing ever fits.

(I am in company, but in waking I will not say
with whom; one will not want to be mentioned,
another will not want to be reminded and the third
   will want to be the hero of the whole story.)

Finally, at the southwest end, the space opens up;
a series of curving balconies, five or six stories
high, frame a sort of rock-walled courtyard.

Jeering neo-Nazis lean over the railings, clad in
yellow satin bomber jackets; we are issued laser
pistols and encouraged to amuse ourselves by
picking them off without legal consequence.

They all plunge forward and down to die, like
nameless, numbered and uncredited henchmen
in old westerns. Strangely, they do not scream
and never seem to hit the floor.

In all the fun, I forget to ask who is keeping score.
The winner gets a green motorcycle, currently
idling just outside the door to the parking garage.
Beyond that, a warm green afternoon awaits.

III. Somewhere in Southeast Wichita, Kansas

Whatever else is to be found here, I have come
for cheap books and a passable Philly cheesesteak
(in no particular order) –

that is, if I can find a parking space somewhere
in these great gray bland acres surrounding the
sprawling temple of commerce.

No one enters or leaves, or perhaps there is a
concerted plan to do so while I am on the far side
of the mall on this endless orbit.

Either way, it looks like rain and I have places
to be, although those places are ill-defined
      and subject to change.

A spot has opened up; no time for the sandwich,
but at least I can pick up some books – if I can
      find them, which looks unlikely.

There are no shelves, only a jumble of boxes
stacked on long plastic tables. Every few minutes,
      the store expands in all directions.

      You should have eaten first,
the lone worker in the store says.
      You're going to be here a while.

IV. Near Kansas City International Airport

I have come from south of the river, leaving
a string of boutique shops more or less near
the River Market, taking an elevated stretch
of most likely Broadway, if I had to guess.

No one can say exactly where the road ends
and the mall starts; at some point sky gives
way to ceiling and blacktop to carpet.

We (all others implicit in this pronoun remain
a mystery) have to get out from time to time,
to carry the car down short flights of stairs; this
will be an inconvenience on the return trip,
      though the lifting itself is not strenuous.

Occasionally, the halls spiral in on themselves;
each time, we barely manage to back out safely.

Finally, we reach the food court, long and wide
and tiled in black and white. No one else is here,
       not even my anonymous companions.

Probably for the best; all the menus are in scripts
I cannot read, and I've forgotten my wallet again.

VI: Hays, Kansas

This place is bigger than I anticipated, four levels
rising from the fringes of the Smoky Hills; must be
good traffic from the interstate. All I want is something
whose name I can never remember; I do recall that
       I want it in blue, if I can find one.

Night comes on quickly here; one minute we shield
eyes from glass-gleam, Kansas sun reflected in
numberless panes, and the next we sit in lawn chairs,
outside a motel from a 1950s postcard, drinking
lemonade from bottles which always seem to be
       three-quarters full. It saves money.

The mall itself has jumped a road and a river beyond,
in the blink between daylight and full dark. It is lit
from within, the malachite color of a vampire's eyes
       just before the fangs come out.

Occasionally, someone inside will come to one of
the thousand windows and wave. It becomes a sort

of game to guess which one will be next.

Beats the crap on TV,
I say, but you have already gone in to bed.

Lenexa, Kansas, Which is Not Really Lenexa, Kansas: Dream I

I should be north of the river right whenever this now
    happens
to be, at a family function of some significance, but it
    seems
more urgent to be here, in this gas station turned
    hardware store
        turned deli, stapling prosciutto to a cutting
    board.

The process leaves more marks than it should, and I do
    not have
        permission to be here; best to move on, I think.

At the Mediterranean market across the street, the
    owner shares
bites of smoked cheese, dusted with Aleppo pepper;
    his spice
room has at least three dozen drawers, inviting a long
    visit to
revel in the swirling chords of scent, but I sense that
    the longer
I stay, the worse it will be for me when I finally meet
    whatever
        obligation awaits me two counties and one
state line over.

One room remains, tables piled high with fruit.
    My hospitable

captor bids me sniff out the lone durian, which has disguised
        itself to hide in a jumble of papaya-watermelon
    hybrids.

                    That one,
I tell him, stabbing out a finger at random; this blind guess
    seems

        correct, or close enough, and I make a break for
    the car.

I have made it north just in time, or so I tell myself, but in
the reception line (for what, I still have no idea) she glares
    sidelong
over a fixed grin as well-wishing strangers pass with glad
    hands.

            Don't ever sing that you'll stand by me,
    she mutters, tears filling the open spaces of her
vowels.
            I know you don't mean it.

Tornado Dreams: or, Behind the Wall Cloud of Sleep

For we're creatures of the wind, and wild is the wind

-Ned Washington

I. Liberal, Kansas, atop the building that was once the Warren Hotel

Someone else is with me, just off my left shoulder,
    moving deftly
and silently to stay out of sight as I turn (and I turn
    often, to see
        whether any of the funnels ringing my town
    have moved);

they spin silently in place, tall thin drab things that might
    be sentries
or siege engines, for all I know. From my left, a voice:

I told you they'd come.

II. Kansas City, Missouri, westbound on I-70 east of Downtown

Coming out of the Benton Curve, I find myself driving
    the wrong way
in the eastbound lanes. with a three-wide twister meeting
    me head-on.

It lifts my car free from the blacktop. I don't think I'll
    be home soon.
        Well,

I say aloud,

this ought to be interesting.

III. Topeka, Kansas, outside an entirely dreamed-up movie theater

A Fujita-4 monster on the right, at least a quarter-mile
    wide; on the
left, a tagalong half its size – which just gives it something
    to prove.

Of course, they would show up the one night this place
    is showing
both *King Kong* and *Son of Kong* in glorious black and
    white.

Neither one seems to be moving that fast, so I might be
    able to get
the first feature in, at least. I hope whichever tornado hits
    the place
        finds a way to spare its pink and blue neon lights.

*IV: Shawnee, Kansas, in a nonexistent church with a domed
    sanctuary*

This funnel breaks through the roof – white, shiny,
    appearing made
        out of plastic rather than wind.

It looks better than what I'm working with now. I grab
    the end of it,
a foot or so back from the mouth, and slap on a wand.
    The tornado

bucks and twists for a bit, but is tamed easily
    enough.

The pews look great; someone else will have to deal with
    the hole
        in the ceiling. I'm only the custodian, not a
    roofer.

V. Liberal, Kansas, near the intersection of Second and Clay

I have never seen a tornado moving away from me,
    until now.
It hops my decrepit stucco house (which might or
    might not
        be real but has never been mine) and moves
    away east.

                That's right — you better run,
I mutter, and chuck a plum-sized hailstone at its back.

*VI. Wichita, Kansas, atop the west stands at Cessna
    Stadium*

The high school track meet paused for the occasion,
    we look
back toward Old Town as God's finger scrawls across
    the city.

Its tip is a gargantuan No. 2 pencil, bright yellow, tip
    slightly
dulled with effort. A pause, a lift, a straight line, a long
        loop.

> *I wonder what it says,*

someone to my left muses.

Whatever it is, we will need satellites to read it, though
    we will
        most likely ignore any inconvenient
commandments.

VII. Northeast of Elkhart, Kansas, along US Highway 56

Well-behaved, these are: a neat file, parallel to the road,
    keeping
all whooshing to a low hum and taking care not to take
    out any
fences or power lines. As each passes me, it stops for
    inspection.

> *Carry on,*

I tell them (over and over, parade and review without end,
    amen)
> *and don't make a mess in Rolla.*

VIII. Kansas City, Missouri, on Grand Avenue Downtown

Gaunt, gray, the twister ducks behind the Power and Light
    Building,
flicking a thumbnail-sized bit of Art Deco shrapnel as it
    goes.

Indiana limestone pings off my left temple, a quick sting
    and trickle.
        It's not the blood that bothers me; it's the
betrayal.

We have an agreement: They get to hide from me while
  I'm awake

        and they're forbidden to hurt me when I'm not.

On top of that, if I can't find that little bit of stone and
  put it back
I'll have to pay for the building, and who carries that much
  cash?

IX. Mission, Kansas Within Sight of Gladstone, Missouri

Work has let out early, perhaps for the storm; when did
  we swap

        glass and steel for an old red-brick schoolhouse?

The Kansas River valley intervenes, as it does, though
  the land
has moved east along with water; I see the church and
  churchyard
at Maple Hill just off to my left. Perhaps the two small
  funnels –

        both white, both wispy – have more power
  than they show.

I suppose I must wait to go north now, though I have
  no idea why
I wanted to go in the first place. The funnels whisper
  from miles

        away, but I cannot decipher their breath-talk.

X. Shawnee, Kansas, Intruded Upon by an Imagined Las Vegas

Clouds go pink, purple, green, yellow, and the twister
spawns in a shower of electric gemstones and casino
bells; in the clouds, a number rolls over.

The funnel touches down delicately, atop a ten-story
cylinder of concrete and steel. Carnival music plays
from the roof, and we all laugh – until the first chunks
             of jagged rubble begin to fly.

There should at least be free drinks, but everyone seems
             to be cutting back these days.

XI. *Liberal, Kansas, Kansas Avenue and Trail Street*

Northeast to southwest; this is not the natural progression,
    but then
again, most tornadoes are not three inches wide and made
    of ice
(fine particles, rounded edges; it does not hurt when they
    hit me).

One by one, they move in over the old Bryant Hotel,
    drop to the street,
come to me where I wait with shoulders back and eyes
    high.

I am where storms come to die, or perhaps to ascend
    straight to Heaven;
        this is a serious responsibility. I might be crying;
    I am not sure.

Kansas City Which is Not Really Kansas City: Dream IX

A warm wet May or June afternoon, gray above and
    green below,
and I have descended to the lowest level of the
    museum; one
long room, open on more or less the west side to an
    overgrown
ravine, a tangle of thin-branched, white-barked almost-
    trees.

It is either the Nelson-Atkins or the Kansas City
    Museum,
though also both and neither, depending upon whether
the thing or things contained in this discreetly lit
    display case
        is (or possibly are)

        a polished white gleaming narwhal skeleton,
        a stylized bas-relief of a narwhal, executed in
white marble
        or
        a matched set of crossed lances, ebony-shafted
and of unknown
            provenance, whose deadly white
points are narwhal tusks.

Each takes a turn in the case, each time I look away.
    I hope it is not my
task to make a final decision; this rain has made me too
    sleepy to think.

New York Which is Not Really New York: Dream IV

Water to the south when I arrive by unknown conveyance,
luggage (contents equally mysterious) in hand. Bearings
gained
> (a lower Manhattan *sans* skyscrapers and traffic,
> which always fails to strike me as strange),

I walk north.
A sign --
> *DO NOT PASS ME BY*
> *I AM HAVING A BAD DAY* --

and now a bus station, familiar from dreams of somewhere
either here or not; things relocate while I am awake, and
> it is no use trying to pin them to any map.

The ticket machine is fussy. It eats eighty-five cents:
my last change. The bills in my pocket bear pictures
> of high-school classmates.

The station operator is friendly but easily distracted.
Nothing remains but to wander outside, behind the station,
into mud flats along a river flowing out from a forest
of strangely shaped trees. like mangroves exposed
> to Strontium-90 or crossbred with waterspouts.

I am called back, admonished not to roam unattended.
The ticket clerk has disappeared. The bus is pulling away.

Liberal, Kansas, and Yet Another Return to My Childhood Not-Quite-Home: Dream I

Grown from 14 to anywhere between 40 and expired,
planting tulips alongside the driveway by the light of
                 either sun, moon or streetlight

(clocks and calendars are not to be trusted; they grow
                 fickle on this side of the wall),

my work – once my mother's, with me relegated to
weeding haphazardly, daydreaming even more so –
is interrupted by a stranger: a woman of equally
indeterminate middle age, with an ever-changing
                 number of young girls in tow.

Their hair is blonde, the color of hay just before the
cut; they wear white blouses, pinafores of Black Watch
                 plaid, low-top red canvas Keds.

                 This is important,
she says in passing, leads her daughters through a new
(or perhaps second) front door which has just appeared
in the middle of the living room window; they all carry
                 long bundles, wrapped in brown butcher paper.

This cannot be allowed; there are things on the dining
room table which no one must see, or the shame would
leave me exiled from this town, from the world itself.

Get out of my house,
I scream at her and hers, though when did it become
mine again? I have no paperwork that I know of, only
a sense of rightful possession and defense.

I threaten her with the police, but she only nods to
the eldest daughter in that moment:
Put them over there, dear.

They have arrived in a brown minivan, parked at
the near curb; I will get the plate number, then call
for backup. I have forgotten whether any warrants
might make this my problem, too.

My pencil is broken; the camera on my phone
produces only blurs. All the while, these cheerful
intruders go back and forth: out from the mystery
door empty-handed, back inside with more bundles.

I grab the mother by the shoulder with one hand,
rip her burden away with the other. It tears open,
falls to the curving sidewalk; she begins to cry.

We are only trying to help you,
she manages to get out between heaving sobs.

She points down, and I see green and gold: beans,
squash, cucumbers, spilled across gray concrete.
The youngest emerges from the house with a
handful of strawberries; one tear streaks her face.

Dream Bill I: I Want a New Flood With
a Girl Like You

An intimate venue: the covered back porch at Jim Roper's
old house northwest of the Kansas State campus,
    somehow
now situated under the west goal of a little high school
    gym
somewhere in the Oklahoma Panhandle. Today, Huey
    Lewis
and the News are either opening for or slowly becoming
the Smithereens, Pat DiNizio having graciously
    resurrected
        for one matinee only.

Stevie Ray Vaughan is here, Schrödinger's bluesman
    (both
dead and not dead until you open the commemorative
    box
set) taking in the show from the bleachers. He's cut his
    hair
and gone a tad rockabilly, matching his three sidemen
(Treble Trouble, one presumes) in Ed Hardy bowling
    shirts,
flames on black. They all laugh often, easily. I hope he
        has arranged ground transportation.

The band slips in from the back yard, launches or rather
lurches into "If This is It." Huey looks cadaverous,
    sounds
worse, but his sax and rhythm guitar player grins and

takes

over the lead vocals. There will be no refunds, either way.

We all – including Roper, yet another returning from
Wherever's Next for the occasion – pitch in by taking on
a share of the background duties.

Ooo-wop,

we sing.

ooh-ohhh,
ooh, ooh, ooh, ooh
let me go …

Maybe, if I'm lucky and the show goes off as expected,
Pat will need a little help with "Blood and Roses" or
"Behind the Wall of Sleep." Maybe I'll call Stevie Ray
up to jam with us. I glance to my left, catch him looking.
I raise my eyebrows, nod toward the stage, mouth

Later, you think?

He nods, says something aside to his band. They do not
laugh, which I take as a hopeful sign. Huey (by now much
recovered) asks us if we believe in love, and through
Roper's

back window I see summer rain begin to fall.

A Suburb Vaguely in Johnson County, Kansas,
Which Might Also Be a City Near You:
Dream I

I seem to be both the youth pastor and
myself, assigned to conduct a funeral
        to gain needed experience;

I wonder why the elders snicker when
        handing down this new duty.

Why the family chose this venue is also
a subject for puzzlement; the departed
lies in repose in either a mall food court
or an airport lounge, reachable only by
a wide staircase, all slick glass and steel.

One misstep, and the pallbearers could
be back within a week as the headliners.

Open casket; he has the face of someone
I remember from Cub Scout Pack 73

        (no, from high school; he was fond of
        wandering supermarket aisles shouting
        Mom Mom Mommmmm
        to see who would come running)

        (no, from a federal courtroom in
        Kansas City; he wore a Marshal's
        badge and a grim focused scowl).

First, a meal; I am late through the line,
last to pick at my salad: iceberg lettuce,
red and yellow grape tomatoes, too much
            store-brand Zesty Italian dressing.

The family watches me too intently; fearful
of choking in my hurry, I send them out to
shop for bargains in black clothing, to watch
airliners land and take off, perhaps to toss
round shiny wishes into fountains. They will
            be paged when it is time to mourn again.

I send for them, not noticing until they
arrive that I am naked; another delay
to put on gray slacks, white shirt, blue
blazer. I have forgotten my tie, or never
had one, or decided I found it garish.

I smile, inviting joy at the prospect of
this departed one's rest in Heaven; all
the living stare, slate-faced, in response.
Of course: If I cannot say who he is,
or was, or has been at any or all given
times, how can I declare where he is?

            (I know him, I would swear,
            but we are taught not to
            swear; let my yes be yes and
            my knowing be no)

Indiana Jones and the Hellgate of Mission, Kansas: Dream I

Harrison Ford is back on the big screen,
all stoic crag and rasp, delivering either
rough order or tough-love chaos to some
red-brick town in red dirt country (scenery
trumping plot, as so often happens, but
            the establishing shots are gorgeous)

and at some point it either ends or starts over
where I came in, my signal to pick up the
            two youngest kids outside the Target.

While I wait, I pass the time apologizing
to strangers for somehow confusing the 2006
World Cup with World War II and claiming
            earnestly to have been at the wrong one.

Something big seems to be happening at
McDonald's; a block-long banner announces
            JIMMY'S COMING!

without further elaboration. Might as well
stop to investigate; there could be prizes.

Jimmy is less who than what: the top half
of an Animatronic android fry cook, wearing
            the crew uniform and a terrifying grin.

An emcee works the crowd, distributing pink
hats whose logos refuse to hold their shapes.
Finally, the question must be asked:

What's happening, Jimmy?

Unseen gears click and hum; mechanical eyes
widen in unholy yet family-friendly joy.

SATAN'S happening!
And French fries!

My son rolls up in a stolen bread truck, pleads
with me to get in. My daughter laughs with her
friends, all dressed in torn pastels like refugees
from some early1980s music video.

Jimmy conjures flame, flips burgers smelling
of tea roses and fumaroles. I weigh the cost of
potatoes and the immortal soul.

Mission, Kansas, with a Brief Visit from
Manhattan, Kansas: Dream I

Lorena from work has a book release party tonight;
she has bound her own copies in a smart subdued
plaid of red, black and blue. She says

> *Everyone has to do this now, to save*
> *money; don't steal my pattern for your*
> *book, either. I'll know.*

Fortunately, the craft store has moved back into its
old location, within walking distance of both home
and office; might as well get my fabric picked out
        before all the good ones get snapped up.

It would help if they kept all the fabric in one place,
        but any help is hard to find these days.

In several of the aisles, shrines have been set up
to various Norse deities; for a brief moment I am
tempted to ask one of them for help, but the whole
        idea does seem a bit ungrateful to Jesus.

At last, between model rockets and color-shifting
paint, I find a bolt of likely-looking print: a soft
sort of jersey, white with blue and green blotches,
        rather like the spots on Holstein cattle.

The title would look good in embossed gold foil,
but they just ran out and I can't afford it anyway.

There is a long line to get the fabric cut; if I don't
mind waiting a little longer, there's a Kansas State
football game going on out back, and tickets are
            free with a minimum purchase of one yard.

I would go, but I promised to stop by Lorena's book
launch and I have a lot of stretching and gluing to
finish after that, with no idea of how to do either one.

Thor has shown up, in response to some frustrated
shopper's petition. He doesn't look so hot these
            days; small children follow him, shouting

                    Santa!

To his credit, he keeps the hammer to himself.

Kansas City Which is Also Overland Park, Kansas: Dream I

It takes a while to place this stretch of street (or rather
streets), with its red-brick antique stores, its hair salons,
its bakery and gallery and anachronous travel agency.

Someone, it seems, has folded the map so as to overlay
45th Street east of State Line and 80th west of Metcalf,
then set it down on a steepish slope, east at the bottom.

Two small white houses, one on each side, sit atop
the street. They are in slight need of paint, but not
so badly as to get letters from either city or both.

This street exists nearly perpetually in early evening;
on rare occasions, you might catch it on a sleepy
Saturday morning. It is always sometime between
late May and early July, and the air often smells
            of hidden roses and imminent warm rain.

The sidewalks are empty, but there is a sun-faded
red pickup – a round-fendered Chevy, something
that rolled off the line in Truman's only full term –
            parked halfway up the hill on the south side.

Whatever might lie to the west, beyond the hill's crest,
I have not seen it. I am not sure that anyone has, aside
from whoever lives in those white houses. Sometimes,
            dark songless birds fly over from that direction.

No matter what time it is, the businesses all closed
five minutes ago. I will have to come back tomorrow.

Hydrocodone II: A Suite in the Key of Silence

I: An undisclosed and unidentifiable location

A long low room, torch-lit and smoky, floor all black
stone but for two squares: one lacquer-red, one gold.

I am made to stand in the red and wait, silently, for one
who is *She* (no further identifier given) to come, to take
Her place in the gold; She will sing and I must follow.
I will know the words, though not what they mean.

She does not come. The gold square fades to black.
I want to ask what this means, but my voice is gone.

II. A flowerbed outside St. Luke's Hospital, Kansas City

Someone (I am not sure who) has been murdered and
buried here; a tall young blonde woman is guilty and
suspects that I know, even though I have no evidence
beyond a decorative post, shaped vaguely like a daisy
on a long white stem, which has been moved slightly.

I push it back into its proper place, and we exchange
looks; I shrug and go to pick up my younger daughter,
who is now two (at most) again. She is dressed for
church, it seems, in a frilly red-and-green dress; her
hair is curly, done up in tiny bows like rosebuds.

I will say nothing, for now; I have her safety to think
about, and I can always come back and dig later.

III. Somewhere in the West Bottoms, Kansas City

I am a smalltown sports editor again, advising a young
writer on a high school track feature; he writes on a
small red plastic device, almost a toy. He must be new.

In a small metal building, near the old stockyards,
a smallish blond boy – pale, crew-cut and with a
pugnacious jaw – is being given a new name and life.

Tomorrow night, he will compete illegally in a junior
varsity football game in Beaver, Oklahoma. I should
report this, but the young writer assures me this is
done all the time; anyway, he says, the football player
is an android and will be disassembled afterward.

My twinge of pity is brief; the pizzas have arrived.

Kansas City Which Somehow is Also Tulsa: Dream I

I wait in the car, in both the East Crossroads and the Pearl,
to be admitted to some great sculptor's presence;

in the meantime, his dogs – one black, one auburn –
lean into the driver's side windows, friendly eyes full of

Memento mori,

keeping watch until it is time to go inside. They lead me
to two-story, flat-roofed red brick, north side of one street
and west side of the other; this means something significant,
according to the slanted evening sunlight.

Denise (from the Sunday school class) is there already and
is to be admitted first; I drag the motorized elevator chair
into the center of the room, check connections, flip the
switch,
watch her disappear. The chair remains.

Shoogy's, one block west, has pretzels or perhaps ice cream
or *Povitica*; there is no sign above the door, but everyone
(in two cities at once and none at all) knows Shoogy's.

I have money, which is not always the case, but no shirt;
people are staring, muttering mockery at my build, and
now
I have nothing to offer when (or if) I meet the great
sculptor.

It is First Friday; to the west, galleries fill and spill onto
sidewalks. Whatever the season was five minutes ago,
    it is
early June now, and a storm builds in the west beyond
    west.

I have not met the great sculptor, but I must go. There
    is a
way home, a retracing of the way into this neighborhood,
            but I cannot remember all the turns.

I am going to be late for dinner, or perhaps to meet
    myself
somewhere on the twisting road that might get me
    there.

The Undiscovered Country Club: Dream I

She is dying – perhaps still, perhaps again – but
        I have promised her this round.

I have not played in decades, and never enjoyed
it that much. Too many triggers – topped irons,
screaming slices, putts pulled *justthiswide*– but
        I have promised her this round.

I wait at the first tee for her to arrive, scout out
the hole: par three, straight, green at the bottom
of a steep slope. The best course seems an easy
swing with a short iron, gravity doing the bulk
of the work if I can keep it down the middle.

A group of six near the green move aside,
inviting me to play through. If I wait, the next
bunch up is a fivesome, each looking every bit
        of eighty-seven and none too spry.

Evening is coming, sooner every minute,
and the light will not hold out long enough –
        but I have promised her this round.

She is here now, and unsteady. All carts
have been rented. If we descend this hill, I
likely will come up alone on the other side.

We sit, wait our turn, watch March sun fall
into night. I know she will rise again, though

not from this bench.

Go on,

she says —

but I have promised her this round.

Backward/Forward I: A Life Ago and the Day After Tomorrow

No point in driving; revelers fill the streets. The car stays
parked up the hill, on Kessler, with hopes it will be there
and intact in the morning. Dusk now, and I have walked
        for seeming minutes and passing years.

Just off the Boulevard, where a lumberyard should be,
a more sanctioned event is under way: sequined dancers,
cheerleaders, thumping bass, a beer tent. Next door,
hawkers in a converted garage sell commemorative
everything for too much money; no good thing is real
        without a T-shirt to prove it happened.

I am accosted by drunks, demanding to know why I do
not smile, drink, shout, drink some more; I flash my ID,
which expired under a bridge some blocks back, but
        they do not look too closely at the date.

At Rainbow, three cars' worth of police have had just
about enough of this; a crowd gathers to dance, thinking
        their red-and-blue lights part of the celebration.

Almost full dark now. My house, when I reach it in a few
more miles and steps, is both itself and not. It rests atop
tall metal bleachers, girders spray-painted some metallic
shade between brown and gold. She has removed the stairs.

                It's okay,
I call up from what used to be the front yard.

The car should be safe, and I can work
from home tomorrow.

She appears at the window, looks down. The porch light
flicks off – then, after forever, back on again.

I need it to get to work,

she says,

but I guess you can go back for it after
dinner. Take the side way up; I'm not
putting the stairs down again tonight,
not with people acting like this.

Stakeout in the Subdivision of the Dead: Dream I

One tree, silver-barked, leaves the size of a man's hand
(the man being either Brandon from the next office over
          or Andre the Giant; there are no in-betweens);

they shift color every six seconds, give or take, a cycle of
basketball orange, ripe-wheat gold, the green of fresh peas.

It stands on a low hill surrounded by gray houses; these
are occupied only by ghosts, but they must be watched.

Brandon and I sit a dozen or so feet up; his branch runs
east from the trunk, mine to the northwest (or so it seems;
          low clouds mask the sun, if it is even there).

We must stay here until we are relieved – by whom, we
          have not been told – and I am hungry.

I break off a leaf in its green phase, roll it, take a bite;
          it tastes of guava and English cucumber.

                    Those things are going to poison you,
          Brandon says.

I pick another leaf, orange this time, and a warmth of
vanilla chai fills the air; strangely, the flavor is that of
the candy cigarettes I would buy at the Jack and Jill on
Second Street, between Sunday School and church.

They haven't caused any trouble so far,

I say.

Even if they do, I'm caught up at work
and one of these houses has to be empty.

Liberal and Olathe, Both Kansas, Neither Really Itself: Dream I

I have a work dinner tonight, or rather the company has
    one:
shrimp and fries at a semi-Cajun chain, followed by bowling.
It is a reward for something or other, and the board is in
    town.

First, my party (having gone to the movies) must somehow
catch Interstate 35 going southwest, from my southwest
Kansas hometown, and wind up in east-northeast Kansas,
in the southwest quadrant of the Kansas City suburbs.
    Consequently, we arrive late.

We try to catch up, snag bowling balls ahead of dinner,
    but
they are picked over; the rejects that remain are yellow,
soft, full of holes. All blame is laid on me, for having been
    born in the farthest corner of Kansas.

Over dinner, we discuss the bravery of the first human to
see crustaceans as food. One person at the table has been
given lobster instead of shrimp; even without the shell,
    I can tell by the size of the claws.

Someone else at the table has written a scathing song, to
a tune I should know, about one of the board members.
If the allegations are true, and she considers us all far less
than qualified, I worry that this is a sort of Last Supper.
    If so, one could do worse.

Before I can pick out shoes, it is announced (loudly)
    that I
have parked badly and must remedy this. I do not recall
having parked at all, and so it takes overlong to find my
    car,
even longer to find a space in the lower level that is not
        taken up by heavy, luxurious furniture.

I have missed out on bowling: All that remains of the
evening is to circulate, assess threats, jockey for what
positions might remain if all dark rumors prove true.

A former intern, brought in for the occasion, insists
    that
all my work is based upon hers. Her eyebrows look like
fan brushes, only black; she arches them to make
    points.

I retreat to the lower level with a cookbook, the cuisine
of a country either overrun years ago or never extant
in the first place. There will be places to sit, to hide, to
wait all of this out. Eventually, I will have to climb the
steep, treacherously narrow staircase, full of hard right
        turns, devoid of handrails.

The book will remain, placed conspicuously on a maple
coffee table so that I do not forget to come back for it.
        I already know that I will forget.

The Oklahoma Panhandle Which is Also the Persian Gulf or Perhaps the South China Sea: Dream I

South and southeast are the new west, as
the gaze flies; either the world has turned
90 degrees to the left, gusting to 135, or all
past mapmakers are proven unreliable.

Three miles away, four at the most, where
Turpin's water tower and grain bins should
rise, spikes of glass and steel rise to pierce
twilight sky; this is either Dubai or Macau,
perhaps both – though, never having been
to either, I should be forgiven my uncertainty.

The highway slopes down, into choppy surf
brown with prairie dirt; on the south shore,
a man rolls up the bridge and puts it away.

> *Shallow enough to walk across,*
someone says,
> *or at least that's what I heard.*

A crowd gathers, urging me forward; at the
water's edge, my friends place winking bets.

One foot in; warm enough, at least, and the
chop is down – then the first fin appears,
and another, and a hundred more, and all
is sleek bodies, flat black eyes, jagged teeth.

I turn to find the same smiles on faces I
thought I knew; in the bleak mirrors of
their gazes, I see the city's lights go red.

Kansas City Which is Not Really Kansas City: Dream XI

I know this gallery space, or these spaces, or most of
either it or them; in an old life, I almost (even sometimes)
belonged in the various heres, as much as I ever could.

Familiar names and works dot red brick walls; familiar
faces move along them, smiles skirting eyes that stare
                    pointedly over my left shoulder, one brow arched.

My shadow stills laughter; where it lifts, so do moods,
                    the knowing corners of wine-stained mouths.

An old couch in a dim side room: This is refuge. Its red
cushions remember my form, accommodate changes
                    undergone over better (or worse) than a decade.

Underneath, a torn leather bag stuffed with relics: photos
of yellow walls, old business cards, press credentials and
                    pay stubs from magazines that never existed.

I lay them out on a white folding table, studying each one
as if seeing it for the first time; wondering who might
still be calling the old number, still writing to an inbox
                    now inaccessible as a government gold reserve.

Lights flicker, conversations fade; time to move on, out
into the gentrifying dark. I would take these mementos
with me, but they cling to the table, and I remember that
sometimes I cut my fingernails too short to be useful.

In Brian May's Parlor, London or Somewhere Vaguely So: Dream I

He is younger again, all gray vanished from
those frizzy locks, neither yet Sir nor Doctor,
though this will change as our time together
rolls on, dilating only on my side of the room.

He brings out the Red Special, the Old Lady,
the Fireplace – not a copy, but the artifact
itself, knitting-needle tremolo arm and all.

He starts to hand it to me, then thinks better
of that; I am, however, allowed a close-up view.

It looks duller, browner in person; one of the
                cutaways seems to have filled in.

                It does that sometimes,
he says, with an apologetic smile and shrug
but no further explanation; the magic of both
earthly and stellar shifts is far over my head.

He begins to age faster now, as he talks of
his father; at irregular intervals, he glances
toward the ceiling with a worried expression.

I hear nothing upstairs; his concern must be
related to something beyond the upper floors,
perhaps the roof, perhaps the stratosphere.

If something upward unsettles an astrophysicist
this much, perhaps I should be going; then again,
who wants to live forever?

Liberal, Kansas, with Easy Access to Faraway Places: Dream I

Everyone has come home for the weekend,
although I am the only one who has lived in
this part of our fused houses; the other two
never had basements.

The utility room has grown while I was not
around to prune it back; it now doubles as the
senior citizens' Sunday school classroom in
a Baptist church in the Kansas City suburbs,
though the washer and dryer can be loud and
disrupt the morning lesson.

Its new twin bed will do for me; let someone
else have my old room across the hall, and be
haunted by the phantom of my potential.

The country club golf course is just beyond
the back fence; I could get in a quick nine, or
even eighteen if it could be cajoled into
becoming the municipal course, but the sun
has fallen pinky-width low to the horizon
and I never much liked the game anyway.

Tomorrow will be busy: a baseball game in
Kansas City, then transporting some great
bulky something or things from vaguely
Ottawa to perhaps Wichita, all before noon,

The load requires a trailer; this will make
the interchange at Emporia tricky, but I or
perhaps a still-unset we will manage, even
if the cargo itself remains unidentifiable.

It appears to be both carcass and appliance
(Is there such a thing as self-freezing meat?)
with a long space down the top for a cord;
whether spinal or electrical, or some hybrid,
it will help to secure the thing for travel.

In the meantime, I will read ghost stories
and dig through this old desk for all the
homework I never handed in; this alone
could take what hours remain of the night.

Steve Brisendine lives, works and remains unbeaten against the *New York Times* crosswords in Mission, KS. A 2024 Pushcart Prize nominee and three-time nominee for the Thorpe Menn Literary Excellence Award, he has appeared in *Modern Haiku, Flint Hills Review, I-70 Review* and other publications and anthologies. His other collections from Spartan Press are *The Words We Do Not Have* (2021) and *Salt Holds No Secret But This* (2022). He doesn't pay submission fees and doesn't think you should, either. He has no degrees, one tattoo and an unironic fondness for strip-mall Chinese restaurants. Write to him at steve.brisendine@live.com.

This project was made possible, in part, by generous support from the Osage Arts Community.

Osage Arts Community provides temporary time, space and support for the creation of new artistic works in a retreat format, serving creative people of all kinds — visual artists, composers, poets, fiction and nonfiction writers. Located on a 152-acre farm in an isolated rural mountainside setting in Central Missouri and bordered by ¾ of a mile of the Gasconade River, OAC provides residencies to those working alone, as well as welcoming collaborative teams, offering living space and workspace in a country environment to emerging and mid-career artists. For more information, visit us at www.osageac.org

Osage Arts Community